# Privilege of Love

### Ashley S. Johnson

Privilege of Love

© 2018 Ashley S. Johnson
Ambitious Artists Publishing

This book or any portion thereof may not be reproduced or used in any format whatsoever without the expressed written permission from the author.

Printed in the United States of America
First printing April, 2018

ISBN-978-0-6921-0123-0

*I dedicate this book to all the sensitive artists around the world.*

*Keep loving and creating!*

# Table of Contents

A Wise Woman ............................................................. 7
Butterfly ........................................................................ 8
Butterscotch ............................................................... 10
Conversation with God ............................................. 12
Change ....................................................................... 14
Hollywood Ain't ......................................................... 15
Imposter .................................................................... 16
In The Light ............................................................... 17
Let Go ........................................................................ 18
Love ........................................................................... 19
Moving Train ............................................................. 20
My ENEMY ................................................................. 22
My Pain ..................................................................... 24
One Night .................................................................. 25
Privacy ...................................................................... 26
Repeat ....................................................................... 27
Shattered Glass ........................................................ 28
Show .......................................................................... 30
Scene ......................................................................... 31
You ............................................................................ 32
Part 2 ................................................................... 33-100

# A Wise Woman

A wise woman holds her head high
And admits when she is wrong
She's a lifetime student
She challenges mediocrity
And uplifts the world
Spreads joy and truth
Has had her heart broken
A time or two or three
Judges no one
Wants evolution of humanity
Equal opportunities for all hues
The chains of poverty broken
Families united
There's no limit to her power
There's no limit to her reach
Even through the fear, she pushes through
Even through the tears, she pushes through
**A Wise Woman** knows that forgiveness heals

# Butterfly

Butterfly, Butterfly, spread your wings
Show off your beautiful colors so the world can see
You're no longer a caterpillar, so don't play small
Your bright colors will change the world
People will stare in awe
The yellow on your wings will attract the bees
But be sure to look out
When you turn your back, they might sting
Don't worry about your missing antenna
Everything has flaws
The green on your right wing
Will surely attract them all
But don't be fooled by their kindness
They want something in return
Just spread your wings and keep flying
Soon enough, you'll learn
I've saved the best for last
And I'm talking about the RED
Love is a part of life
It brings healing and peace
But never underestimate it can also bring defeat

You now know enough to travel the world
Show off all your colors
And be proud of what you are
A beautiful **Butterfly**

# Butterscotch

When you walk in a room
You set the bar high
Your good looks and your charm
Damn boy you fine
In your three-piece suit
You'll turn any woman's head
Your butterscotch skin
And your almond brown eyes
Enough to make me faint
And provide a natural high
Everyone in the room is watching you move
Smell so good, ooh weeee you just sent
 me to the moon
Okay... I'm back, staring into your beautiful eyes
Oh, but wait, you pull out another surprise
Those beautiful pearly whites
Baby, you got me swooning over you
Feeling like a schoolgirl
About to turn into an
Animal at the zoo
I'm undressing you
And I don't care who's watching
And all this happened in ten seconds before you could

Ashley S. Johnson

extend your hand to say Hello
I'm in love with you, **Butterscotch**

# Conversation with God

**Me:**
I'm a fighter
But I'm tired
Where are you
I need you

Feeling alone
No place is home
Do you hear me
Tell me the truth

I need you to show up
And show out
Can't take no more
Just hear me out

**God:**
I'm your Father
Listen to Me
I'm right here
I'll never leave
Give it some time
You're not alone

Do you hear Me
You must believe

I'm here to show up
And show out
Give me your heart
We'll work it out

**Me:**
I'm sorry
I love you
I'll never doubt
I know the truth

**God:**
I forgive you
You're My child
I'll never leave
You make Me proud

# Change

Love is like a moving shadow
I can't seem to catch
I've been chasing it for years
Guess it's not ready to be
captured yet

I've chased it East to West
Then West to East
Feeling like I'm in a tornado
Fighting my way back to peace

I've been sucked up
Thrown around, then thrown
away like garbage
Body mangled with cuts and scars

And still, my heart is open and ready for true love
I will pick up these pieces and everything I've lost
Including me, it's time to rebuild
No more excuses, it's time for **Change**

# Hollywood Ain't

So many lost souls
So far away from home
Big dreams and shooting stars
Drugs and broken hearts
The land of the free

Hollywood Ain't what it seems
People pretending to be
What they're not
To get their spot
Everybody needs to come clean

Its time fly high
Above rejection and pride
Lean on Him
He'll get you through
Open your heart
And you won't lose

**Hollywood Ain't** what it seems

# Imposter

Love me like you used to
When your heart was full
Full of love for me
And no one could pull
Your heart away from me
What happened to those days
When I was your true love
And you were my Professor
We would laugh and joke
Until we were in pain
Laughter slowly turned into silence
When you revealed your other side
Lying and cheating, all I could do was cry
I mourned the death of the man
I thought you were
He disappeared 6 months ago
and now I'm left with
An **Imposter**

# In The Light

I'm running in circles trying to find me
Damaged heart, who can see my real parts
Love on the line, more like needing a lifeline
My world's breaking, I find solace in Him

When will I get my shooting star
My King of Kings with healing scars
My bright light and freedom ringing
Rebel in the night
Fragile in the light

I'm running in circles trying to heal myself
Broken spirit, dodge the truth and everyone's help
Love in the air, more like needing air
My world's shaking, I find solace in Him

When will I get my shooting star
My King of Kings with healing scars
My bright light and freedom ringing
Rebel in the night
Fragile **In The Light**

# Let Go

I need your love like I need air
Many times, I wonder if you even care
Your heart is cold, your words are few
I need to hear I love you
My heart aches when you aren't around
You call me your Queen
But you've stolen my crown
Broke it into pieces
Or you've given it away
Sometimes, all I can do is close my eyes and pray
Pray that I heal from the hurt that you've caused
Deep down, I know that we all have flaws
I've asked God to give me a sign
Are we meant to be or am I holding on too long
It hurts me so much to see you leave
I know in my heart we could never be
I'm just being selfish, holding on to a dream
We never stood a chance
This I know
Lord, please give me the strength
To just **Let Go**

# Love

Unlock the pain in my heart with your key
Let it float away, never to return
Flood my heart with love and joy
Not that fake ish
That wake-up smiling love
That breakfast-in-bed love
That purpose-driven love
That kingdom love
That unconditional love
That see you at your worse
But love you to your best love
That I'm taking you home to mama love
That I'll wait for sex until marriage love
That I'm going to make you my wife **Love**

# Moving Train

It hurts to let go, but I know I can't stay
We break each down with our words
When we know that's not God's way
We should've ended this a long time ago
But for selfish reasons, we decided to struggle
Struggle with a false reality
That has only caused pain
Constant arguments that continue
To drive us both insane
My heart is growing cold but
can the damage be reversed
Sometimes, I feel like I deserve it
Or possibly I'm cursed
I knew from the beginning that we could never be
I was too afraid to be alone
I'd rather lie and deceive
I woke up today, and I just can't lie anymore
I wish I could've have told you sooner
I've tried before
Our romance is now in a casket
I want to cry and scream
I just don't have the strength to patch it
Patch this lie, that I've been keeping a secret

Time to move on, I know that we both need it
My heart is crying to be set free
I can no longer ignore
What my intuition is telling me
You're not the man for me, I'm putting God first
I must save us from ourselves
before life gets any worst
This is my goodbye, no more see you later games
I must unbuckle this seatbelt and get off this
**Moving Train**

# My ENEMY

Got me feeling alone and scared
Creeping into my thoughts
Somehow got my vision impaired
Judging my life
And the mistakes that I've made
Telling me to go down one path
When you know it's a trade
A trade where once again
I get the short end of the stick
Just LEAVE ME ALONE
I know I can fix it
You tell me my dreams aren't real
And that they'll never come true
I guess they never would
If I were conniving just like you
YES, I finally got it straight
You're trying to break me
Drag my name through the mud
So everyone else will hate me
Let me leave my legacy
And allow my light to shine
No, we cannot co-exist
Your fears are greater than mine

You're afraid of my success
And if I'll still want you
Or if I'll turn my back
Ridicule and taunt too
I'm here to tell you that
You don't really exist
And those times I stayed up worrying
Late nights when you were pissed
You're no friend to me
And I don't need you as a crutch
No, let me finish
YOU talk too much
You've done enough damage
And I can't fight you anymore
No more let's get even
Or try to settle the score
You've fought me with all the weapons you own
But you can't get rid of me
My light shines too bright so
You're no longer **My ENEMY**

# My Pain

My Love
My King
My Everything

When I fall
I know You're here
To rescue me
You have my heart

When I'm alone
And I can't see
I know Your love
Will heal me

I will never
Let You Go
My heart may break
But still, I know

You are worthy
You are great
You're the conqueror
Of **My Pain**

# One Night

Sweet and strong
Hard and tight
Tall and beautiful
But only for one night

Vibrant and fun
Charismatic and smart
Loving and kind
But only for one night

Confident and ambitious
Knowledgeable and free
Curious and satisfying
But only for one night

Cultured and creative
Talented and bright
Charming and sexy
But only for **One Night**

# Privacy

I cried, I prayed, I fought with all my might
But still, our love could not withstand
The cheating and lies left me broken and bruised
I tried so hard, but you never did
You just wanted me to forget and forgive
Yes, I forgave you
But the pain was drilled into my core
You never stopped to pull out the stake
You drove into my heart
Instead, you twisted and turned it
Pounded it even more
Broken and alone, you acted as if your life was grand
You could not empathize with the pain you caused
Six months ago, I was your queen
I was living a fairytale lie until I invaded your **Privacy**

# Repeat

Eyes meet
Souls rejoice
Dinner for two
Hands held
Lips touch
Family met
Finger shines
Vail lifted
Cheers heard
Paradise reality
Dreams shared
World traveled
Lovemaking
Baby Bump
Growing love
Baby crying
Beaming smiles
**Repeat**

# Shattered Glass

Putting together this broken glass
Is becoming too much
I'm tired of my fingers bleeding from all these cuts
I'm picking up each piece and you're just
Standing and watching
Every time I put the glass together
You step on it again
You walk away laughing, look at me,
Then shake your head with disgust
Can't you see I'm bleeding to death
From all these cuts
What happened to the man that
Loved and protected me
He disappeared in the middle of the night
And never returned
I kept staring out my window
But you never came back
You left me with these pieces
But it's time to give them back
I'm giving back all the pain that you've caused
It's just too much
Your lying and deceitfulness have crushed my spirit
No longer will I sit and cry, I'm taking my life back

Won't sit in these insecurities
I'm releasing myself from this trap
You can keep your **Shattered Glass**

# Show

Where is my story
I've been waiting all along
I'm a writer and so much more
But what will be my song
You created me uniquely
And for this, I am grateful
Time to step into my purpose
This is God's **Show**

# Scene

What hurts the most is you didn't fight for me
You let me slip away into a loveless world
A place where I've shed a thousand tears
Not a tear in sight for you
How is it so easy for you to sit
On the sideline and observe
As if you're watching someone else's movie
This was supposed to be our happily ever after
I guess you missed that **Scene**

# You

I never knew love
Until I met you
Your fire, your passion
Were so new to me
I heard many speak
Of the joy they found in You
I couldn't grasp that concept
Until You placed your hand on my heart
I want to love
Just like You
I want to forgive
Just like You
I want to heal
Just like You
I want You
No, I **NEED You**

# PART 2

My heart isn't made of stone
It breaks
It hurts
It bleeds
It heals

I drank from the fountain of love
That he offered me
It turned out to be a fountain of poison

We danced under the stars
Listening to John Coltrane and Miles Davis
At that moment, I knew it was love

Hold my waist
And pull me close
Run your fingers through my hair
As we watch the moonlight dance
On the dark sea

Never give up
On your soul's desires
Let your heart lead the way

Man will never
Know how far
He can go
Unless he simply
Goes

Our time is now
Our time has always been
Too bad
That you are just
Waking up
To our magic
That radiates
From within

Time doesn't exist when I am with you

In the end
We always have
The truth
Love and Light

Show me your truth
And I'll show you mine
Let's create our world of love
Never let go

I have a heart
Or did you not notice
After you disappeared
The first time
I gave my love to you
I have a heart

I was never enough for you
You didn't know
How to love me
And you didn't care
To learn

I fell in love
With a guy
He fell in love
With me
Then, he fell in love
With my friend
I hope they're happy
In the end

I am enough
In my raw nakedness
Deliberately, I create
The life I desire
Love, joy, growth, and freedom
Will you join me

**Big dreams
Became
My misery**

**Courage
Became
My victory**

Ashley S. Johnson

**Life without love
Is not a life worth living**

Fireworks when we kissed
Fireworks when you held me
Fireworks when we laughed
Fireworks when we dreamed

I was born to love you

...always

The heart speaks
Until you listen
It will not give up
Until it is free
Free to love
Free to simply
Be

You must listen
To your soul's desires
It will free you
From suffering and pain

I waited by the phone
But you never called
I sent you love and kisses
Both were met with ice
I gave my whole self to you
Only for half to return
Lesson Learned

Ashley S. Johnson

The genie granted me
One wish
He told me
I could have any treasure
In the world
I wished for more time
With you

# Privilege of Love

In the fall, I fell in love with you
In the winter, you held me close
In the spring, our love blossomed
In the summer, we became one

Sometimes, the gift is hidden in an ugly box
Don't be afraid to open it

I am praying for you
My King
I am dreaming about you
My King
I am sending my love to you
My King
I am patiently waiting for you
My King

A cup of Love
A cup of Laughter
A cup of Adventure
A cup of Freedom
A cup of You
A cup of Me
Makes the perfect Us

Our history
Torn apart and tattered
Lost and devalued
But still, we smile
Our hair
Kinky and free
Mocked and copied
But still, we smile
Our love
Dysfunctional and passionate
Fiery and painful
But still, we smile

Ashley S. Johnson

My heart is lonely
I long for your touch
Please come away with me
I'm ready now
But will you ever return
I want you, your laughter, your smile
My favorite baller
My favorite chef
My favorite companion
My true love
My Forever Love

Raindrop soothe my heart
Drip drop through the night
Take me to another plane
Where the sun shines through the rain
Flowers glow in the dark
No one wonders where to start
Spirits flying in the air
Never fear, always prayers
Wash away my sins
Wash away my pride
Cleanse my heart
Open my third eye

I can see the pain
In your eyes
It's hard to ignore
I can feel the break
In your heart
Yearning to explore
I can hear the fear
In your voice
Releasing the inner war
Yes, I see you
And I still want you
Mi amour

Take hold of my heart
And gently bathe it with your sun

You said you would answer my questions
But where are you now
I've been asking since day one
And no answers have been found
Yeah, I get it, you said you wanted me to fly
Figure out things on my own, let my ego die
The inner struggle is real
I find myself questioning my existence,
Relevancy and appeal
My heart is so easily pained
Why can't I just say
Forget them all and remain sane
If I did that, I wouldn't be me
Your Daughter, Queen, Maker of History
I must admit, turning the other cheek is hard
But if Jesus could do it
I will heal these scars

Her strength is unmatched
But she doesn't feel like being strong
She laughs to keep from crying
She smiles to hide her pain
She closes her eyes to escape time
Where will she go
What will she do
Her heart is in a million pieces
Who can put it back together
Who will tell her it's okay
Who will tell her to breathe
HE WILL

I loved you when you were broken
But you couldn't do the same
I took on the world for you
Until you were free from the pain
I prayed for you and cried with you
Only to be left nearly insane
But still, I wouldn't change a thing

In your presence, I am free
In your presence, I am me
In your presence, I am whole
In your presence, I am never alone

Place your hand on my heart
Feel my love
Can you see that I adore you
I've dreamed about you
I've prayed for you

I see you
Is what he said to me
Turns out
I wasn't the only one
He saw

Love is the answer
To some of life's
Toughest questions

**You loved me back to life**

I fell in love with a Cancer
He treated me like a Queen
Everything was great until
He cheated on me
I fell in love with a Leo
He called me Beautiful
Everything was great until
He cheated on me
I fell in love with a Virgo
He told me I was the One
Everything was great until
He cheated on me
I fell in love with a Sagittarius
He called me Luv
Everything was great until...

Thank you for letting go
When I couldn't
Thank you for being cold
When I wouldn't
I'm better off now

My soul cries when I think of you
You were a precious gift that I couldn't keep
One day, we will meet again

I know that you're hurting
I know that you're lost
I know that you drink
Yourself to sleep
Avoiding life's scars
Open up to me
I only want to love you

I see your brilliance
I see your power
I see what you could be
I see what we could be

Left turn
Right Turn
Wrong Turn
And still, I found
You

He was a talented artist
He was a star
He was a lover
He was a lie

I was falling for you
While I was still
Loving him
I stopped answering
Your calls
You stopped calling
I left him
And now you're
With her
Now, life's a blur

I'm afraid you aren't for me
And I am not for you
Let's not waste our time
Trying to explore
And create faux chemistry

She's still waiting for you
And he's still waiting for me

I escaped the city
Only to find
That my heart
Stayed in the city
Where dreams
Manifest
Purpose is
Found
I'm happy to say
I've located my
Crown

Give me a
Pina Colada
On an exotic
Beach
When these
Tears
Won't stop
Flowing
Down my
Cheeks

In all my brokenness and pain
You still saw the REAL ME

You prefer money and power
You leave a trail of broken hearts
Glad I wasn't your next victim

You're perfect on paper
But still
You weren't perfect
For me

I'm not impressed with your
Penthouse
I'm not impressed with your
Cars
I'm not impressed with your
Clothes
Let me see your
Scars
Who turned your heart so
Hard

When I am with you
I feel like I'm on another plane
Soaring and floating
All at once
I don't want this feeling
To ever go away

**The impossible became possible with you**

A love that heals
A love that is pure
A love that doesn't judge
A love that doesn't hurt
A love that brings peace
A love that brings joy
A love that hypnotizes
A love that soars
A love that isn't afraid
A love that is bold
A love that is free
A love that protects

He's the only one who truly gets me
He's the only one who truly cares
He's the only one who truly sees me
And I love Him

Love at a funeral
On a cold dreary day
You showed up
To love me
In every single way
You embraced me
And didn't quite know
What to say
But your love
at a funeral
Is what I'll remember
Always

Our love was
Like popcorn
Delicious when cooked
The right amount
Of time
Disgusting when burnt


...You can never fully get rid of the stench

Ashley S. Johnson

Raisinets and popcorn
Is the memory
I recall
But it was always
So much more
Than just raisinets and popcorn

Can we act
As if the past
Doesn't exist
Can we start over
With our first kiss
Or maybe with
Our first carnival trip
You won me a fish
How easy is this

Love,
Eight

...our fish 🐟

Your words stung
Like a dagger
In my heart
Never did I believe
That you would be him
And he would be you
And we would no longer
Exist

M was a charmer with gorgeous eyes
E was an artist and loved life
J was my heart and soul surprise
R was a friend and unlikely teacher
O was my weakness and strength
J was my hardest lesson to date
Oh, how I once adored them all

You did everything
You said we would
But only without me
Harsh reality

My only regret
Was being afraid
To love you
As you were

You were a King in my fantasy
Turns out you were the Frog
I had to Kiss
On my way to the castle

Perfect peace and love is my gift from You
Love and joy is my gift to the world
You chose me and, in turn, I choose You

www.ingramcontent.com/pod-product-compliance
Lightning Source LLC
Chambersburg PA
CBHW050916160426
43194CB00011B/2432